CITY MACHINES
CHERRY PICKERS

Connor Dayton

PowerKiDS
press.
New York

Published in 2012 by The Rosen Publishing Group, Inc.
29 East 21st Street, New York, NY 10010

First Edition

Editor: Jennifer Way
Book Design: Ashley Drago

Photo Credits: Cover, p. 16 © www.iStockphoto.com/Joe Potato Photo; pp. 5, 11, 12 Shutterstock.com; pp. 6, 15, 24 (bottom right) iStockphoto/Thinkstock; pp. 8–9, 24 (top left) Bob Carey/Getty Images; p. 19 Andy Sotiriou/Getty Images; pp. 20, 24 (bottom left) © www.iStockphoto.com/Joe Gough; pp. 23, 24 (top right) © www.iStockphoto.com/ David Jones.

Library of Congress Cataloging-in-Publication Data

Dayton, Connor.
   Cherry pickers / by Connor Dayton. — 1st ed.
      p. cm. — (City machines)
   Includes index.
   ISBN 978-1-4488-4960-4 (library binding) — ISBN 978-1-4488-5070-9 (pbk.) — ISBN 978-1-4488-5071-6 (6-pack)
   1. Cherry pickers (Machines)—Juvenile literature. I. Title.
   TJ1363.D385 2012
   621.8′73—dc22

                                  2010050459

Manufactured in the United States of America

CPSIA Compliance Information: Batch #WS11PK: For Further Information contact Rosen Publishing, New York, New York at 1-800-237-9932

CONTENTS

Cherry pickers lift people into the air. There they do many jobs.

People use cherry pickers to work on **power lines**.

Firefighters use cherry pickers. They can get them close to a fire safely.

9

A person stands in the bucket. The arm lifts her.

12

The arm is also called the boom.

Some cherry pickers are part of a truck. They are called bucket trucks.

15

16

The first cherry pickers helped people pick fruit in trees. That is how they got their name.

The bucket has controls. They move the bucket up, down, and sideways.

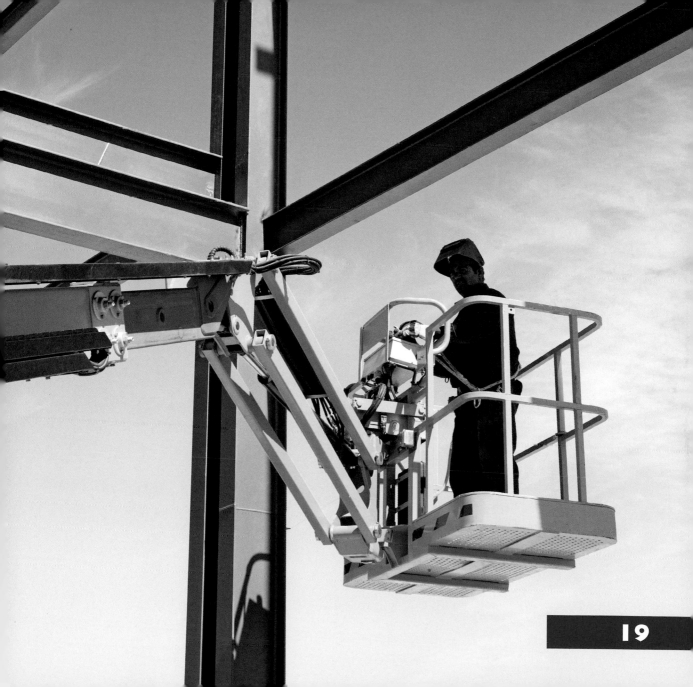

19

The person in the bucket wears a **harness**. This keeps him safe.

Workers must also wear **hard hats**. These are for safety, too.

23

WORDS TO KNOW

firefighter

hard hat

harness

power lines

INDEX

WEB SITES

Due to the changing nature of Internet links, PowerKids Press has developed an online list of Web sites related to the subject of this book. This site is updated regularly. Please use this link to access the list:
www.powerkidslinks.com/city/cherry/